GRAVE-ROBBERS, CUT-THROATS AND POISONERS OF London

First published in 2002 by Watling St Publishing
The Old Chapel
East End
Northleach
Gloucestershire
GL54 3PQ

Printed in Thailand

ISBN 1-904153-00-3

24681097531

Cover design and illustration: Mark Davis
Cartoons: Martin Angel

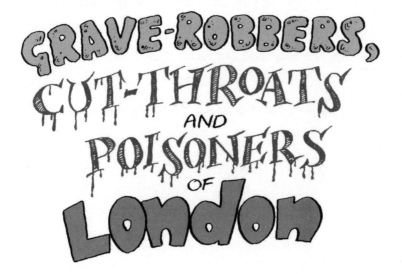

GRAVE-ROBBERS, CUT-THROATS AND POISONERS OF London

Helen Smith

WATLING STREET

Helen Smith lives in Brixton with her daughter. She is the author of two highly acclaimed novels, *Alison Wonderland* and *Being Light*.

This book is for Vanessa, Zachary and Francesca

Contents

Pickpockets, Beggar-masters, Princes and Kings

Girls and Boys Wanted!

Would you like to make lots of money?

Are you brave?

Are you quick to learn?

(If not, you'd better be really good at running)

Interesting job available for the right applicant. Come to the Spotted Dog Tavern in St Giles and be prepared to pass a series of tests.

[Note: You must be willing to share the money you earn. The management accepts no responsibility if you get caught and hanged]

What would you think if you saw a notice like this? Would you be tempted to apply? Would you know what you were letting yourself in for? You'd better read on ...

In the 1600s, 1700s and 1800s pickpockets worked in pairs on the streets of London. They usually belonged to gangs of thieves, which were controlled by people known as beggar-masters or captains, who taught them to steal, then sold what they stole, and kept some of the money they made in return for food and a place to stay. The masters always had a favourite tavern or pub that they used a bit like an office, selling whatever had been stolen that day. This made it easy to find them, if you wanted to join their gang, so there was never any need for advertisements like the one on the page before (and anyway, only half the population could read and write at the time). All you had to do was turn up in London and ask around.

There were two main reasons why anyone would want to join a gang of thieves in London:

1) They'd heard thrilling stories about the adventures of thieves with nicknames like 'Prince of Pickpockets' or 'King of Fences'.

2) They were poor and hungry and couldn't think of any other option.

The Prince of Pickpockets

George Barrington was known as the Prince of Pickpockets in the 1770s. He was a well-dressed, well-spoken man who had trained as a surgeon. As he left church one day, he was arrested and

found to be wearing several pairs of trousers in order to conceal the valuables he had stolen. He was asked to remove his hat, and when he lifted it up very, very carefully, a watch fell out from under it, which he said he'd found lying on the ground.

Because of his elegant appearance and his education, George Barrington could move unnoticed among the crowds at the theatre, in churches and even in the Houses of Parliament. He was responsible for the theft of a fabulously expensive diamond snuff box, said to be worth £32,000, which he took from the Russian Count Orloff while he was at the theatre.

The King of Fences

A fence was someone who bought and sold stolen goods. He or she was often the rich and powerful head of a criminal gang who was respected – or feared – in their local neighbourhood. Ikey Solomon was a well-known fence with a vast network of thieves working for him in the 1770s. He was based near Petticoat Lane, where lots of second-hand and stolen property was traditionally bought and sold in the market. For ten years until 1826, when he was arrested, Ikey was known as the King of Fences: the most powerful of all the powerful figures in the underworld at that time. He was so well known that when Charles Dickens wrote

Oliver Twist in 1837–8, about a boy who is tricked into joining a pickpocket's gang run by a man called Fagin, he based the character of Fagin on Ikey Solomon.

You would probably never think of leaving home to go and join a gang of pickpockets. I know I wouldn't. Imagine trying to survive on the money you made from stealing, going hungry if you didn't do very well at it, and living with the fear of being caught and hanged. But in the 1600s, 1700s and 1800s adults and children who were poor or desperate came to the taverns in London to find the beggar-masters. They hoped for a better life than the one they'd been born to. They were often disappointed. The beggar masters were horrible people who were only interested in making money from their gang. They would even turn one of their own gang in to the law if they didn't make enough money for them.

Two Beggar Masters Who Were Women

Mother McCloud lived in London in the 1770s. She trained young pickpockets, including her son Peter, who was hanged for stealing in 1771 when he was only fifteen years old. 'Tell my mother not to be too upset,' said Peter. 'I hope I'm going to Heaven.'

In the 1800s Mother Cummins lived in St Giles, a notorious slum, or 'rookery' near the Seven Dials area, where lots of criminals lived. Mother Cummins rented out rooms and bought and sold stolen property. She also taught boys to pickpocket and she used young girls to tempt drunken men to her house, where she robbed them.

(You've probably already guessed that they weren't called 'mother' because they were nice, kind, cuddly ladies. It was just a name, like 'Mrs', that was used for women in those days.)

Joining a gang

If you wanted to join a gang of thieves, you first had to pass a series of tests, like snatching a wig from someone's head, or a watch from their pocket.

There's a story about a boy of fifteen called Harvey Hutchins who came to London from Shrewsbury in 1693, hoping to join a gang of pickpockets. Harvey had been an apprentice to a silversmith but he'd been caught stealing from him and he was put in prison and whipped. Harvey was so impressed by the stories he heard about London thieves from some of the other prisoners, and particularly about a beggar-master called Constantine, that he decided to find him and join his gang. He met some young pickpockets in Islington who told him to look in the Dog Tavern in Newgate, which was run by a man called Snottynose Hill. Sure enough, Constantine was there. He showed Harvey a silver tankard he'd stolen from a tavern in Cheapside. 'I'll take you on as an apprentice if you steal another one just like it,' he said.

'Can you run, master?' asked Harvey.

'I've outrun hundreds of people in my time,' boasted Constantine.

'Good, then we shall have that tankard,' said Harvey, who had come up with a rather risky plan.

When they got to the Cheapside tavern, Harvey asked the landlord if he remembered losing a silver tankard and pointed at Constantine. 'There's the man who stole it!' he shouted. Constantine looked horrified and then started to run. While the landlord chased after Constantine, Harvey reached behind the bar and stole a second tankard.

Constantine was furious when he met up with Harvey again later that evening. 'If they'd caught me, I would have been hanged,' he said.

'I knew you could run fast,' said Harvey. 'And after all, I passed the test.'

Constantine took him on.

Criminal Classes

• Few criminals lived past their early twenties. Poor Harvey Hutchins lasted until he was twenty-six years old before he was caught and hanged in 1704. He had worked for Constantine for years and, after setting up on his own, he was caught breaking into a house.

14

• If you passed a test and the beggar master took you on, you'd spend about three months in a kind of apprenticeship with the gang, learning their tricks and proving that you were good enough to join them.

• In *Oliver Twist*, Charles Dickens describes how Fagin teaches Oliver to steal a handkerchief from his pocket by pretending it's a game: 'See if you can take it out, without my feeling it, as you saw them do, when we were at play this morning.' He loads up his pockets with watches, jewellery and purses and makes the other boys in the gang practise stealing from him without him noticing it.

Artful Dodgers

Jack Dawkins, alias 'the Artful Dodger' was a cheeky boy in Fagin's gang who 'had about him all the airs and manners of a man' and was as 'swaggering a young gentleman as ever stood four feet six, or something less.' Perhaps, when he was writing about the Artful Dodger, Charles Dickens was inspired by stories he'd heard about boys like these:

Jack Goodwin, alias Plump, was caught stealing 150 guineas from a gentleman's pocket in 1699, when he was eleven years old. He was hanged in 1706, when he was still only eighteen, but even so, he managed to cram plenty of cheeky tricks into his short lifetime. He stole the bottom out of a silver tankard so that the next time the landlord used it, the beer flowed and flowed but the tankard never filled up. He dripped warm wax on to a companion's eyes so that they could beg for money by pretending he was blind. Plump stole the money they had made and threw his 'blind' friend into a river, where he stood until he was rescued by passers-by. (Don't you try the trick with warm wax under any circumstances, it will burn you and could blind you permanently.) When Plump was finally arrested he was carrying rope and his accomplice was carrying a pistol, but they claimed to be tailors. 'You use very thick thread,' said the magistrate, eyeing the rope. 'Oh yes, I generally use very coarse cloth,' said Plump. People in authority don't like it if someone makes a better joke than the one they've just made. Plump and his friend were hanged shortly after this conversation.

Dick Low started stealing in 1693. He too was only eleven years old. He and other young thieves like him, who went into people's homes and took whatever they could pick up and run away with, were nicknamed 'St Peter's children'. This was because St Peter, one of Jesus's disciples, was a fisherman, and those young thieves were so good at stealing, it was almost as if they had a fish-hook on the end of each finger. Dick Low was hanged in 1707, when he was twenty-five years old.

Tom Taylor was a young pickpocket of about the same age as Dick and Plump, when he went to Drury Lane one evening in about 1675. He put his hand into the pocket of the gentleman sitting next to him and stole 40 guineas from him. He was delighted at getting so much money so easily, and he went back the next day, wearing a different set of clothes. He sat next to the same man, thinking he wouldn't be recognized. But when he slipped his hand into the man's pocket, he couldn't get it back out again. The man had sewn fish-hooks all around the opening of his pocket. Perhaps he was sick and tired of having his pocket picked by 'St Peter's children' and decided to teach them a lesson. Tom struggled to release his hand for about fifteen minutes, and all the time the man said nothing, he just sat back and watched the play. Eventually Tom said, 'Sir, I appear to have put my hand in your pocket by mistake.' The man got up, still without saying a word, and walked to the nearby Rose Tavern, dragging Tom with him. Tom managed to get a message to some of his friends to bring 80 guineas – double the sum he'd stolen the night before – to pay the man to release him. Even when he'd paid up, the man was still angry, and started beating him with a cane. A crowd that had gathered chased after Tom once he was free, and ducked him in a horse-trough so roughly that they broke his arm. Tom gave up being a pickpocket and turned to stealing from people's houses instead. He made it to twenty-nine years old before he was hanged, in 1691.

William Cox was caught stealing several times but each time he managed to escape being hanged, perhaps because he was short and slim, so he looked young for his age. His appearance was also useful for committing crimes. Dressed

17

smartly in clean clothes and carrying a bag of marbles with him, he invited the children of shopkeepers or the sons of rich people in grand houses to play with him. This gave him a chance to go into the houses and shops and steal or get information about what was inside, which he passed to a thief called Captain Davis, who would return later on and rob them. One day William took a tame sparrow with him into a house that belonged to some kindly old people. When they found William there, he burst into tears and told them he was looking for his lost pet. They ran around trying to catch the bird, before realizing that William was making off with their possessions in the meantime. William's young face couldn't keep him from the gallows forever. He was hanged in 1773.

Criminals used a kind of slang called 'cant' when they talked to each other. There was a thief called Arthur Chambers, who was hanged in 1706 and who loved showing off by using the language in front of people who didn't understand it. He sometimes even pretended he was speaking Greek. Here are some of the 'cant' names given to different kinds of criminals. Would you have guessed what he was talking about, if you'd walked into a tavern and overheard Arthur Chambers's conversations with the landlord? See if you can match the names to the descriptions.

1. wiper-puller

2. moon-curser

3. pudding shammer

4. footpad

5. angler

6. cutpurse

7. fence or black dog

8. housebreaker

9. highwayman or highpad

a) a boy carrying a lamp who made money from showing people the way along dark streets, in the days before electric lights made it easy to see where you were going. These boys would often lead unsuspecting people into dark alleys where gangs of thieves waited to ambush them

b) someone who survived by stealing food

c) a thief who worked on horseback, holding up coaches

d) someone who specialized in stealing lace handkerchiefs

e) someone who burgled houses

f) someone who bought and sold stolen property

g) a thief who worked on foot

h) someone who stole their victim's purse or moneybag by cutting the strings that tied it around their waist

i) someone who sat on a roof with a fishing rod and stole things – like wigs - from passersby

How many did you get right?

Answers: 1d) 2a) 3b) 4h) 5i) 6h) 7f) 8e) 9c)

Tom's dog

A pickpocket called Tom Gerrard had a lovely, friendly dog that he had taught to steal from people and then run back to him with their purse in his mouth. Tom was hanged in 1711, and the poor dog wandered the streets looking for a new master. Luckily he was a pretty-looking dog and he was soon adopted by an old gentleman who was a vicar. When the vicar went out to buy some tobacco one day, the dog ran off and brought him back a purse he'd stolen. Then he ran off again and brought back another one. The vicar didn't realize the dog had been trained to steal. He was so shocked by his behaviour that he took the dog home and gave him the punishment he'd have got if he'd been human – he hanged him.

The sad truth about being a pickpocket (especially if you weren't very good at it):

· If you failed the day's task, you'd go without money and you'd go without food.

· If you kept making mistakes, you'd get hungrier and hungrier and start to get weaker and weaker.

· If the master thought you were really useless, you'd have to go along and spy on the others, to make sure they were handing over everything they stole.

• If you were really, really useless the master could just turn you over to the law to be hanged. (It didn't matter how young you were – you could be hanged for pickpocketing anything worth more than a shilling.)

• If you were really, really, really useless you'd get caught while you were stealing, and you'd be hanged anyway.

Adults and children who were recruited on the streets of London by the beggar-masters were soon discarded if they didn't earn enough money. It was a hard life and a short one, whatever the songs and stories said. Unfortunately there were more pickpockets who ended up dying like Tom Gerrard's pretty little dog than living like princes and kings.

CHAPTER TWO

Jonathan Wild, the Thief-Taker General

Q) What should you say if someone takes your favourite possession and won't give it back until you've paid them some money for it?

A) How much money would you like? Are coins OK or would you prefer notes?

You wouldn't say that, would you? You'd report them to a teacher or tell someone in your family. They'd never be able to get away with it.

Life didn't work like that in the 1700s.

If someone had something stolen from them in the street, or from their house, they didn't have much chance of seeing it again, even if the thief was prosecuted. They could go to the taverns where the beggar-masters sold stolen property, and try and buy it back. If not, they could go to people who had set themselves up as 'thief-takers'. These were private policemen, also known as bounty-hunters, who used to earn money by capturing thieves and turning them into the law for a reward.

The thief-takers used to advertise in the newspapers, or write to people who had been burgled or pickpocketed, and ask for a reward to return their possessions. But most of the thief-takers were mixed up in crime themselves and, even if they weren't directly responsible for stealing things in the first place, they encouraged the people who did steal them. The thief-takers behaved more like villains than like policemen. And the biggest villain of them all was Jonathan Wild, who advertised himself as the 'Thief-Taker General'.

More about Jonathan Wild

• Jonathan Wild was born the son of a Wolverhampton wigmaker in about 1682.

• He was apprenticed to a buckle-maker in Birmingham when he was fifteen.

• He was sure there was more to life than buckle-making.

• When he was twenty, he left his wife and child and moved to London to work for a lawyer. He tried to get to know as much about the law as he could, even though he was only working as a servant.

• The lawyer sacked him and Jonathan ended up owing money.

• Jonathan was put in prison for debt and spent four years in Wood Street Compter, where most criminals were first brought before being sent to other prisons around London. He got to know lots of people that way.

• The people he got to know in Wood Street Compter weren't very nice.

• Most prisoners couldn't afford lawyers and couldn't even read or write, so they were impressed by Jonathan's legal knowledge.

• Jonathan learned about the criminal underworld and how it worked from the other prisons. He also learned cant, the criminal slang we looked at in Chapter One.

• When he got out of prison, Jonathan set himself up as a thief-taker, working for a city marshal (an early kind of policeman).

• Jonathan Wild advertised himself in the newspaper as 'Thief-taker General'. He walked around London carrying a silver stick as if he was a marshal. The stick was a symbol of authority, a bit like the silver star badge worn by marshals in the

American Wild West. He also wore a wig, rode around in a grand carriage pulled by six horses, and carried a sword. He tried to appear outwardly respectable in spite of all his crimes.

• He had a ship that went between England and Holland and Flanders to dispose of stolen property.

• He sliced off his girlfriend Mary's ear with a sword.

As you can tell from reading these facts, Jonathan was a clever man who learned very quickly – whether it was learning about how the law worked from his employer, or learning how to break it from his fellow prisoners. He was also a nasty man who treated his girlfriend badly but on the other hand, as you can tell from the wig, the carriage and the silver stick, he wanted to give the impression that he was a wealthy, respectable gentleman.

Jonathan Wild's Lost Property Office

Like other thief-takers, Jonathan provided a 'service' to people who had been burgled – he returned their property to them, for a reward. He was more successful than all the other thief-takers had been because he was more organized. He wrote everything down.

Most of London's thieves went to Jonathan when they had

stolen something, so that he could sell it for them. Their victims went to his 'Lost Property Office' at his house in Newgate and told him when they'd had something stolen, so he could get it back for them. This way Jonathan had information coming from both sides and he seemed to know everything that was going on in London's underworld, which made him very powerful.

Jonathan didn't just gather information. He also controlled and employed thieves, like a beggar-master acting on a very grand scale, or like a modern-day mafia boss. It was said that most of the 7,000 or more criminals in London worked for Jonathan Wild directly or indirectly. Everyone knew his name and they were very frightened of him.

If Jonathan didn't like someone, or if they refused to work for him, he could soon get enough information about them to get them hanged – and claim the £40 reward or bounty money at the same time. He sent 100 people to their death with the information he had gathered about them.

Jonathan sometimes turned in people who had worked for him. He rode on the front of the carts that took them on the long ride from Newgate (where the Old Bailey is now, near St Paul's Tube) to Tyburn (where Marble Arch is now) to be hanged on the gallows, shouting, 'Make way for my children.'

Double-crossed!

When Jonathan was making notes about the people who worked for him, he'd put a cross next to a name if he had enough information to convict someone. When he turned them in, he put another cross next to their name. We still use the expression 'double-cross' today to describe a betrayal by someone we trust.

Jonathan Wild's friends:

There is a very interesting expression that wise people like grandmothers sometimes come out with: "You can tell a person by the company they keep." Has your grandmother ever said that to you? It means that you can get to know a lot about someone from the kind of friends they have. What do you think Jonathan Wild's grandmother would have thought of his friends?

Charles Hitchin was a marshal whom Jonathan worked for when he first came out of prison. Charles was the master of a group of young pickpockets nicknamed 'The Mathematicians' and taught Jonathan everything he knew about thief-taking. Jonathan and Charles fell out with each other and published angry booklets listing each other's bad points. 'The thief-taker is a thief-maker,' wrote Charles Hitchin. Jonathan called him 'a cowardly lump of scandal', 'ambassador of Beelzebub' (Beelzebub is another name for the devil) and much, much worse.

Quilt Arnold and Abraham Mendez were Jonathan's deputies and bodyguards. They were supposed to prevent crime on the roads going north and west out of London but instead they menaced and stole from the people they were supposed to protect. Quilt married Jonathan's wife as soon as Jonathan died.

Obidiah Lemon was a highwayman – a thief who stole at gunpoint from people travelling in carriages on the highway. He met Jonathan Wild in the Wood Street Compter prison and later acted as an informer for him. Obidiah Lemon is a great name, though, isn't it?

Blueskin Blake was a thief. Blueskin was one of Jonathan's 'foster children' whom Jonathan had found wandering hungrily in Covent Garden and introduced to a life of crime. Blueskin ended up in prison, sentenced to death on false evidence from one of Jonathan's men. Jonathan gave Blueskin money in prison and got him a doctor because he was wounded. When Jonathan visited him with some books to read, Blueskin slashed Jonathan's throat with a knife, almost killing him.

Jonathan Wild's Notebook

(Top Secret – Keep Out)

Blueskin

X   X

Top three most interesting stories about Jonathan Wild

1) The Red Lion Tavern

Jonathan Wild used the Red Lion tavern in Clerkenwell and the house next door to store stolen property, forge coins, interrogate enemies and meet friends.

The buildings had secret doors, trapdoors and hidden rooms. There was even said to be a secret passageway to Newgate Prison. Dead bodies were thrown through the trapdoor into the Fleet River, which flowed outside and was used as London's main sewer at the time (it has long since been covered over). More than 100 years later, when the tavern and its neighbouring house were being rebuilt in 1844, instruments of torture and the remains of dead bodies were found in the basement, as well as a knife with 'J Wild' engraved on it.

2) Training Criminals

Jonathan Wild hired dancing masters for some of his criminals, so that they could learn the manners of the elegant upper classes and would be able to mingle with them before stealing from them. (How organized and sophisticated is that?) Footmen were the best people to be trained for this job because their job was a bit like being a waiter in a grand private house. This meant they knew the way that people in polite society behaved and there was no danger of them giving themselves away by picking up the wrong cutlery or swearing in front of a duchess. It also meant that, as they'd lived among very rich people, they developed expensive tastes and often turned to crime to try and fund a lifestyle beyond their means.

3) Bullet Holes and Scars

Lots of people tried to put an end to Jonathan's power – not just Blueskin Blake. There were nineteen bullet holes and scars from swords and knives on his body, and his skull was held together by metal plates. You can see his skeleton today at the Royal College of Surgeons in Lincoln's Inn Fields.

From the age of about thirty until his death in 1725 at forty-two, Jonathan Wild ruled the underworld. He closed down rival gangs and turned in anyone who refused to work for him.

When he was finally charged with receiving stolen property – a relatively modest £10 piece of lace – he was sentenced to be hanged. He didn't want to face the humiliation of being driven through the streets in an open cart on his way to Tyburn to be hanged, but his request to be driven there in a private carriage was refused.

Jonathan wrote to King George I asking to be spared the death penalty. 'If I receive your Majesty's royal favour of a reprieve, I do firmly resolve to relinquish my wicked ways.' The King ignored him.

The night before he was due to be hanged, Jonathan drank laudanum, which was a strong painkiller made from opium mixed with alcohol. He meant to kill himself but he drank too much and was sick, so he survived. Two of his fellow prisoners walked him up and down in prison, trying to stop him from falling unconscious. They managed to keep him alive.

There were thousands of people waiting to see Jonathan

hanged. Some of them made fun of him by jumping on to the cart taking him from Newgate to Tyburn and shouting 'Make way for our father' (just as he shouted 'Make way for my children' as he led his victims to the gallows). People lined the streets and threw stinking, rotten eggs and fruit at him. If there was a dead dog or cat lying around, they picked it up and threw that as well.

After years of living as an arch-criminal, Jonathan Wild was dead. He was hanged, half-conscious, covered in vomit, wearing his nightshirt. But at least he had his wig on. Everyone celebrated his horrible end and lots of articles and books were written about him. There was just one problem. Can you guess what it was? It slowly dawned on people that they had nowhere to go to get their lost property, now that Jonathan Wild was gone!

CHAPTER THREE

Jack Sheppard's Great Escapes

Jack Sheppard was one of the few thieves in London who refused to work for Jonathan Wild. Jack was hanged in 1724 when he was only twenty-three, after an eighteen-month crime spree and four daring escapes from prison. Jack had become a popular celebrity. Plays, a pantomime, and lots of songs were written about him. Daniel Defoe – who wrote *Robinson Crusoe* - visited him in prison shortly before he died, and wrote an account of his life. Jack even had his portrait painted by a famous artist who was the King's portrait painter, and hundreds of copies of the picture were sold to the public. Over 100 years later, in Victorian times, there were complaints that all the children in London had heard of Jack Sheppard, even though half of them couldn't tell you who the queen of England was (it was Queen Victoria, of course.)

The reasons Jack Sheppard was so popular

· He lived recklessly

· He died young

· He died bravely

· He made FOUR ingenious escapes from prison

· He was funny

· He had a sweet, gentle face

· He was only 5ft 4" tall and he had a stutter

· He didn't care about money

· He never killed anyone

· He never hurt anyone

· He never betrayed his friends

· He rescued his girlfriend from prison

· He loved his mother

· He refused to work for Jonathan Wild

· Did I mention he was funny?

Jack Sheppard's ingenious escapes from prison

Jack had trained as a carpenter, which came in very useful for breaking into houses as well as escaping from prison.

One In April 1724, Hell-and-Fury Sykes, one of the footmen-turned-criminals who worked for Jonathan Wild, had lured Jack into a trap. He'd invited Jack to play skittles with him in a tavern near Seven Dials in Covent Garden but when Jack turned up, the 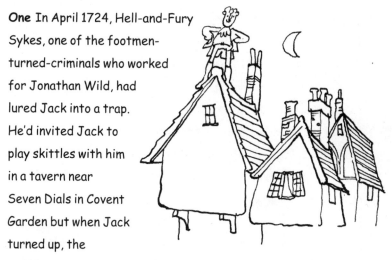 magistrates were waiting there to arrest him. Jack was taken to a prison in St Giles nearby. He used the blade of a razor to carve a hole in the roof, tied his sheets and blankets together, and lowered himself down on to the streets below. One of the tiles Jack had dislodged from the roof hit a man on the head. The man started shouting that a prisoner was escaping, so a small crowd gathered to try and see who it was. Jack managed to get down from the roof without anyone seeing him, by showering the crowd with more bricks and tiles, and then he crept among them. He couldn't resist nudging the man next to him. 'Look,' Jack said, pointing up to the roof', there he is, do you see him?' The crowd started pushing and shoving each other, shouting and pointing, trying to get a better look, and Jack slipped away.

Two In May 1724 Jack was caught for stealing a gold watch and was taken to a prison in Soho. His girlfriend, Edgworth Bess, tried to smuggle him the head of a spear to help him escape but she was arrested and they were thrown into prison together in Clerkenwell. Jack's friends managed to get some tools to him and he sawed through the chains on his legs and Bess's legs, and the bars at their window. He tied their sheets and blankets together and the two of them climbed 25 feet to the yard below. Bess was quite a plump girl but Jack managed to heave her 22 feet up the prison wall and over the top of it, and then they jumped to freedom and instant fame below. Jack had rescued Bess from prison once before and it was generally considered admirable that he hadn't left her behind to rot this time.

Three Jack was arrested again and was awaiting trial in Newgate as the annual Bartholomew's Fair took place in Smithfield in August 1724. Edgworth Bess and her friend Poll Maggott visited Jack and passed him some of their clothes to dress up in. Jack removed an iron bar from his cell window and wriggled through it to join them. The three of them then walked boldly out of the prison together, through the crowds at the Fair, to Blackfriars Stairs, where Jack paid a waterman 7p to row him up the river to Horseferry in Westminster, still wearing his leg irons. The next day Jack slipped into another disguise – a butcher's blue tunic and white apron – and went to hide out in the countryside.

Four Back in Newgate again, Jack was chained to the floor of a cell known as 'The Castle' because it was impossible to escape from. He was hoping to get his hands on some tools which would have been 'more useful than all the silver mines in Mexico' but all he had was a bent nail. The night that Blueskin Blake slashed Jonathan Wild's throat with a knife, in October 1724, Jack made his fourth and final break for freedom. He used the nail to pick the padlocks on his handcuffs, prised his leg irons from the floor, then climbed up the chimney and into a disused room called the Red Room. He broke his way through five more locked doors, got into the chapel, and then climbed down a wall and on to the roof of a nearby house. The roof was too high to jump from, so Jack went back the way he came – through the chapel, through the six doors, down the chimney and into his cell, and he got his blanket. Then he went all the way back again and used his blanket like a rope to climb down from the roof of the house. This amazing escape made the front page of most of the newspapers. Jack was a celebrity and London was buzzing with news of his most daring escape yet.

Jack was on the run for the fourth time in six months. He was wanted by the Law, recognized by most of the criminals in London, feared by most of the shopkeepers, with a reward advertised for his capture, and he faced certain death if he was returned to prison. What should he have done? If you'd met him and you could have given him one piece of advice, what would it have been? What would you have done?

Maybe Jack should have gone to another part of the country and stayed hidden but he couldn't resist having fun. Even when he went to the country disguised as a butcher the last time he escaped, he'd got bored after three days. Here's what he did:

He disguised himself as a beggar and walked around town, listening to the stories people were telling about him in the taverns and even joining in their discussions. He joined the crowds listening to ballad singers. These singers made money from selling, for a penny a sheet, copies of songs based on stories in the news. There was a story about Jack in the newspaper pretty much every week and the ballads were all about Jack Sheppard, as you'd expect. 'The company was very merry about the matter,' Jack told Daniel Defoe.

He went out stealing again.

On his last day of freedom, Jack dressed up in the fine things he'd stolen, including a wig, two pistols, diamond rings, a silver sword and a suit made of silk. He and two girls called Kate got drunk in a tavern and then drove past Newgate, the prison he'd recently escaped from, in a horse-drawn carriage.

That evening Jack visited friends all over town and then met up with his mother, who had been to St James's Palace to try and ask the king to pardon her son, and drank brandy with her in a tavern. Everyone begged him to be careful because he was bound to be captured as he was so easily recognisable.

At midnight Jack was arrested while drinking in a tavern with a girl called Moll Frisky. 'My senses were quite overcome with the quantities and varieties of liquors I had all day been drinking,' admitted Jack. 'I was altogether incapable of resisting.' He was too drunk even to fire the pistols he had stolen the night before and he was hauled off to Newgate for the last time.

A hero's return

Jack was locked up in Newgate again, his wrists and ankles secured with chains that weighed 300 lb, which is about 135 kilos, or more than twice what Jack himself would have weighed. The jailers kept finding tools that friends had smuggled in to him - one friend visited with a Bible that concealed a small tool called a file, capable of sawing through chains. Others brought him carpentry tools; a hammer and chisel, and more files. When the keepers found Jack walking around his cell without his chains one day, he showed them how he had picked the lock with a nail.

A thousand people visited Jack in his first week back in

prison, including Daniel Defoe and James Thornhill, who painted his portrait. Everyone had to pay 4 shillings a visit – a shilling more than the jailers charged people to visit less popular prisoners.

Thousands of people lined the streets to cheer Jack as he came past on the cart on his journey to be hanged at Tyburn, including weeping women carrying flowers. Even when he was on his way to be hanged, Jack was still hoping to escape. A small knife was found on him that he'd been planning to use to cut the rope that tied his hands, and then jump off the cart and run away. But the knife was useless. Jack was such a notorious escaper that he'd been handcuffed with metal chains instead of a rope.

Two sad stories about Jack Sheppard

1) Jack Sheppard and Blueskin Blake broke into William Kneebone's house in the Strand. Mr Kneebone, a kind man who had taught Jack to read and write when he was a boy, visited Jonathan Wild's Lost Property Office to ask for help. Jonathan went straight round to see Jack's girlfriend, Edgeworth Bess. He took her to a tavern for the the evening and bought her lots of drinks, to try to find out where Jack was staying. Bess was very fond of Jack. She had introduced him to his life of crime and he had twice helped her escape from jail. She didn't mean to tell Jonathan Wild that Jack was staying at Blueskin's mother's

house. The very next day Jonathan Wild's deputy, Arnold Quilt, went there to arrest Jack. Jack fired a gun to defend himself but it didn't work properly and Arnold Quilt took him off to prison. Bess helped Jack to escape from Newgate but he never forgave her for betraying him to his enemy. (Mr Kneebone, on the other hand, 'could not refrain from shedding tears' when he came to see Jack in prison and tried to get the keepers to take some of the chains off him.)

2) Daniel Defoe, the famous author, hatched a cunning plan to rescue Jack from hanging. It would be the ultimate escape – an escape from death itself. Daniel Defoe hoped to try to revive Jack after he had been hanged. People were hanged for fifteen minutes, which wasn't always long enough to kill them. There were stories of people waking up on the surgeon's table just as they were about to be cut up in the interests of medical science. Jack was only 5ft 4", remember, and he was very slim. His body wasn't heavy enough to break his neck as he fell from the scaffold, so he would have slowly, slowly choked to death. Daniel was hoping that Jack's body would be too light to pull the rope tightly enough around his neck to kill him. Daniel and his publisher, Mr Applebee, were going to take Jack away as soon as he was cut down from the scaffold, and try to bring him back to life. But the crowd couldn't bear to watch Jack slowly choking for fifteen minutes. They swung on his legs to break his neck and stop him suffering. This wasn't unusual: friends often did this when someone was hanged. It wasn't the first time a rescue

plan had been foiled, either. People sometimes tried to swallow a short hollow pipe to keep their airways open when the rope tightened. But a broken neck's a broken neck and it will kill you even if the rope doesn't. When Daniel Defoe's men tried to take Jack away, the crowd rioted, thinking Jack's body was going to be taken to the Royal College of Surgeons and cut up by the doctors. They refused to let anyone take his body, and took him to a tavern called the Barley Mow for a wake, then buried him themselves at midnight in St Martin-in-the-Fields's churchyard in Trafalgar Square.

I can't help thinking that even if Jack had escaped with Daniel Defoe's help, he'd have been up to his old tricks again, swaggering through the crowded streets of London, drinking in the taverns, laughing and joking and stealing. He loved the attention and the adventure. And sooner or later, he'd have been caught again.

But there is another possibility, isn't there? Perhaps the crowd who tried to protect him had a plan of their own. Maybe the body they buried so quickly belonged to some other poor soul who had died that evening. Maybe Jack escaped on a ship bound for America or Australia or Canada and started a new life there. What do you think?

CHAPTER FOUR

Moll Cutpurse and Jenny Diver

Girls have typically had less freedom and a poorer education than boys throughout history. Even when they grew up, women's opinions were considered unimportant and they weren't allowed to vote until 1918, and then only if they were over the age of 30 (equal voting rights were finally granted in 1928). And it wasn't until 1977 that a law was passed giving women the right to earn as much as men for doing the same jobs.

A lot of women in the criminal world used to make money by buying and selling property that had been stolen by their boyfriends, or by stealing from drunken men who paid them for their company. But two well-known thieves, both called Mary but born more than 100 years apart, were famous as thieves in their

own right. They took two very different approaches to life in a man's world:

Mary Frith – known as Moll Cutpurse – dressed and behaved like a man and insisted on dealing with men on their own terms.

Mary Young – known as Jenny Diver – used to trade on her femininity to trick both men and women and steal from them.

Mary Frith alias Moll Cutpurse

Mary Frith was born the daughter of a shoe-maker in the Barbican in the City of London in about 1589, when Queen Elizabeth I was on the throne.

Instead of sitting around the house quietly sewing, as she was expected to do, Mary preferred playing with boys, climbing trees, swimming in the Thames, running about and fighting. She really liked fighting.

How Mary Frith became known as Moll Cutpurse

Moll is a short form of the name Mary.

She started working as a pickpocket and a cutpurse. Cutpurses usually worked in pairs, with one of them distracting the victim and the other cutting the victim's purse strings. They did this using a 'horn-thumb', which was a sharpened piece of animal horn worn on the thumb like a claw, and which cut through purse strings quickly and easily, even before the victim knew what had happened.

How Moll Cutpurse became known as a Roaring Girl

Moll Cutpurse started dressing in men's clothes and went out drinking most evenings. It wasn't unusual for women to go into taverns and drink but Mary laughed and talked with men as their equals, and she even fought them sometimes.

Tobacco had been introduced to England in Queen Elizabeth's reign by Sir Walter Raleigh and Moll was very fond of smoking. She smoked her tobacco in a pipe, as cigarettes hadn't yet been invented. A picture of Mary dressed in men's clothes was used for the front cover of a play about her life in London called *The Roaring Girl*. Moll, on top of her other aliases, became known as a Roaring Girl.

Roaring Girl dressing-up kit

Here's what Moll would have needed to transform herself into a Roaring Girl:

A set of men's clothes, including breeches and jacket

A pair of boots

A hat

A pipe

A pistol

A tankard – to hold some beer

A deep voice (optional but apparently Moll was noted for having one)

Moll's career path

Moll Cutpurse was caught and had her hand burnt four times as a punishment for stealing. In the end she decided to become a highwayman instead of a pickpocket.

She must have been very successful because when she was finally caught, she could afford to pay a bribe equivalent to about £500,000 to avoid being hanged.

When she was about fifty, Moll decided to become a fence instead of a highwayman. Thieves called 'heavers' sold her account books they'd stolen from shops. The shopkeepers needed the books to send out bills to customers and paid highly for their return. (On top of her other nicknames, people started referring to her as the High Directress of crime.)

Moll Cutpurse avoided the gallows and died in her sleep in 1663, at the age of seventy-four. She must have been a very successful fence because she built stores of gold worth £1 million.

She'd spent the whole lot by the time she died!

Two stange stories about Moll Cutpurse

1) When she was a child, Moll's uncle found her tomboyish behaviour so alarming that he put Moll on a ship that was due to set sail for America. Once they were aboard, he decided to try to 'cure' her by drilling a hole in her forehead. This popular remedy, called trepanning, was supposed to take pressure off the brain by making a hole in the skull. (Incidentally, there was no anaesthetic available at the time.) Moll fought him off and jumped into the sea. Her days of swimming in the Thames came in useful after all and she got herself ashore safely. It was shortly after this that she embarked on her life of crime.

2) When she was working as a fence and dressing as a man, one of Moll's enemies had her charged with wearing indecent clothes. Her punishment was to stand in a white sheet during a Sunday morning sermon. Considering she had been burnt four times in the hand, captured when a highwayman, released, celebrated on stage and pictured on the front of a book, wearing a sheet in front of a crowd didn't bother her at all. Her  friends got their own back on the crowd that had gathered to stare at Mary by sneaking around behind them and cutting bits off their clothes.

Two even stranger stories about other women who dressed as men

1) A woman called Mary Hamilton (yet another Mary!) who lived in Dorset married fourteen different women until finally she was thrown into prison in 1746 and whipped to discourage her from doing it again.

2) Sarah Stanley left her lazy, idle husband in Warwickshire and came to London where she dressed in men's clothes and found work in the House of Commons. She then joined up as a trooper in the Cavalry, where she made such a good soldier that she was promoted to Corporal, until it was discovered that she was a woman. She was honourably discharged in 1796.

Mary Young alias Jenny Diver

Mary Young ran away to London from Ireland with her boyfriend in the early 1700s, when she was about fourteen or fifteen years old. Her boyfriend was arrested for stealing when they reached London and transported to Australia.

Mary found a room to rent in Covent Garden and was introduced to a gang of thieves based in the slums of St Giles. She was so impressed by the amount of money they were able to make in a few hours of stealing that she decided to try and join them.

How Jenny Diver got her name

Mary spent two hours every day learning how to cut purses from people's waists, dip her hand into their pockets and steal their watches. The thieves who were teaching her were impressed by her dedication to their trade. They called her Jenny Diver and they let her join them.

Four stories that made Jenny famous

1) Jenny and the members of her gang often went to church. But they weren't interested in the sermons or the hymns – they were interested in the congregation's money and valuables. Jenny had a special costume designed that made her look pregnant. It had false arms and hands coming out of the sleeves of her dress so she could steal without anyone noticing. One elderly lady who had her watch stolen in church remarked that it must have been taken either by the devil or the pregnant lady

sitting next to her – and she knew it wasn't the pregnant lady because she'd been able to see her hands in her lap all the time she was sitting there.

2) Standing among the people outside church one day, Jenny put out her hand so that a young gentleman wearing a diamond ring could help her through the crowd. As he turned, he realized his ring was gone.

3) Jenny collapsed on the ground near a group of people waiting outside St James's Park to watch the King go by. She was dressed  in her pregnancy outfit. People gathered around her and tried to help her as she lay there moaning, pretending to be in pain. While she was carrying on like this, the members of her gang went around stealing. They got two diamond buckles, a gold watch, two gold snuff boxes and two purses.

4) One day while Jenny was out with her boyfriend, who was dressed as her footman, she pretended to be ill and knocked on the door of a nearby house asking for help. She lay on a couch and picked the pocket of the lady who owned the house as she tried to help Jenny recover by waving smelling salts under her nose. Meanwhile, downstairs, her boyfriend was stealing the silver from the kitchen.

Jenny was eventually caught and sentenced to be transported to America. She was rich by then and she took so many boxes of stolen property with her on the ship that she looked like a grand lady going on tour. She didn't like America because she didn't make much money from pickpocketing, so she sneaked back to London.

Jenny was soon arrested for stealing again but she managed to avoid being hanged by giving a false name, and instead she was transported to America again.

Jenny came back to England a second time, with the help of a man who had fallen in love with her. She stole everything he had and abandoned him when they reached England.

Jenny was finally executed in March 1740. She was given the privilege that Jonathan Wild had asked for, and was denied – she was allowed to ride to the gallows in a private coach.

Jenny Diver combined her skill in pickpocketing with a little acting talent and a lot of nerve. She played on the idea that women were helpless and weak and she used it to her advantage. She charmed and exploited every man she met, from the Irish

boy who brought her to England for the first time to the American man who brought her there for the last time. Moll Cutpurse, on the other hand, was a loud-mouthed, roguish, rough-and-tumble fighting creature with an eye for business and the good sense or good luck to stay away from the hangman. Which one of the two would you rather have been?

CHAPTER FIVE

Grave-Robbers

Imagine you're walking past a London graveyard late on any moonless night in the years between 1750 and 1832. You might see a horse and cart parked outside the gates, the driver looking nervously around, anxious to be off across town with whatever load he's waiting for. You might look through the railings in the graveyard and glimpse groups of men in dirt-covered clothes, moving quickly between freshly dug graves, carrying lanterns that hardly shed any light. If you peer harder into the darkness, you might see two of the men coming towards you carrying a long basket. They stumble. Perhaps they stumble because of the darkness, or because they're drunk or because they have something heavy inside the basket. Whatever the reason, now's your chance to run ...

Before we get to the grave-robbers - here are eight interesting facts about dissection ...

1. William Duell murdered a woman called Sarah in 1740 and was hanged for it. But he wasn't quite dead when he was cut down from the scaffold. To everyone's surprise (including his own), he woke up again while being washed on the surgeon's dissecting table. His life was spared and he was fortunate enough to be transported instead of being hanged again.

2. John Haynes also regained consciousness on the dissection table, this time in 1772. He was taken back to Tyburn and hanged until he was well and truly dead.

3. William Harvey, the surgeon from Bart's hospital who discovered in 1618 that blood circulates through the heart, dissected both his father and his sister (after they were dead). This was extremely unusual – few people ever volunteered to be dissected in those days.

4. Every year, until 1752, six particularly villainous criminals were sentenced to be dissected by surgeons after they had been hanged, as an additional way of shaming them.

5. The demand for corpses for anatomy classes was so great that in 1752 a new law said that everyone who had been hanged for murder should be taken to the Company of Surgeons' Hall, to be dissected there, or passed on to the hospitals and private medical schools.

6. In 1775 the Company of Surgeons (which later became the Royal College of Surgeons) took delivery of the bodies of eight hanged murderers from the gallows at Newgate.

7. In 1826, nearly 600 bodies were dissected in anatomy classes in London.

8. There weren't enough hanged murderers to go round.

Imagine this:

Your father's a doctor. You come home one evening to find him in the sitting room wearing a blood-spattered apron. He's cutting up a dead body on a table, watched by a group of students who are pushing and shoving each other to get a better view of what's going on. Your dog is under the table licking up the blood and any bits of flesh that fall on to the sawdust on the floor.

Surprised?

Not if it was 200 years ago (especially if you'd just come back from a walk past the local graveyard). There were so many medical students in London eager to learn about how the body worked that surgeons set up private schools in their homes to teach anatomy, using dead bodies for their demonstrations. Even the dog's behaviour wouldn't have been a surprise – some hospitals allowed dogs to 'mop up' after operations on live patients.

John Hunter

A surgeon called John Hunter started teaching anatomy in his house in Covent Garden in 1746. He was so successful that he built a house, a museum and an anatomy school in Great Windmill Street in 1770. His students had the luxury of a corpse each to cut up, instead of just watching their teacher do it. When the dead bodies were finished with, they were thrown into a well at the back of the house and covered with chemicals to dissolve them.

There used to be a zoo at the Tower of London. When the animals died, John Hunter was given their bodies, which he stuffed and put into his Hunterian Museum at Windmill Street. The first giraffe seen in Britain was displayed there, and Queen Charlotte also gave him two of her dead elephants.

The sad story of Charles Byrne, the Irish Giant

Charles Byrne was said to be 8ft 4" (2.54m) tall. He earned his living by appearing as 'The Irish Giant' in freak shows at London fairs. Adults paid half a crown to see him, children paid a shilling. He died in June 1783 when he was twenty-two years old.

Charles knew that there were surgeons in London who would want to dissect his body after his death but he didn't want that to happen. Before he died, he paid some fishermen £50 to put him in a lead-lined coffin and bury him at sea.

John Hunter paid the fishermen £500 not to put Charles in a lead-lined coffin and bury him at sea.

You can still see Charles's skeleton in a glass case at the Royal College of Surgeons, along with other exhibits from the Hunterian Museum. It's 7ft 8" (2.3m) tall.

Grave-robbers

Gangs of men started stealing bodies from graves in the late 1700s, to supply the demand for fresh corpses to dissect in the medical schools. They were known as grave-robbers or body-snatchers.

They were also sometimes called 'resurrection men' - because they made dead bodies rise up from the grave after death.

A Grave–robber's handbook:

· After bodies have been buried in the ground for a few days, they start to decompose and were no use to the surgeons in this state.

· The grave-robbers preferred working in winter to summer because the bodies stayed fresh longer (for the same reason we keep food in the fridge) and because the nights were longer – so they had more time to work.

· Moonlit nights were no good, because the grave-robbers could be seen. They used charts to calculate when the moon would be full, so they'd know when to go out to the cemeteries and when to stay at home.

· They used specially adapted lanterns that shone on the ground but didn't illuminate their faces.

· If the bodies had started to decompose, the grave-robbers sometimes just cut off the hands and feet, or pulled out the teeth, and sold those instead of a whole body.

· A lot of people couldn't afford coffins and buried their dead in a piece of cloth called a winding sheet or a shroud, and put them straight into the earth.

· It was quick and easy to get bodies out of the graves, particularly if they didn't have coffins. Grave-robbers usually worked in pairs and could get up to eight bodies in a night, although sometimes they came back empty-handed.

• The grave-robbers went to graveyards if they heard a funeral had taken place, and they gathered information from grave-diggers or the carpenters who made coffins for the hospitals. If they had no specific information, they went out anyway and had a look for fresh graves.

• The body was put in a hamper or basket, and either taken to the private room of a tavern where bodies were bought and sold, like the Fortune of War in Smithfield, or taken direct to the medical schools.

• The grave-robbers knocked on the doors of the medical schools with (not very secret) code words along the lines of 'Do you want anything?' which meant they had a body to sell.

• The grave-robbers were often drunk. This was probably because
i) They had a lot of money to spend, so they spent it on drink.
ii) The job they did was creepy, disgusting and shameful, so they drank to dull their feelings.

A gang of Lambeth body-snatchers, who stole from thirty cemeteries in the late 1700s, charged two guineas and a crown (£2.35) for an adult corpse. Children were sold by the inch – six shillings for the first twelve inches (30cm) and nine pence an inch (2.5 cm) on top of that. They charged more for people with unusual medical conditions.

A dying profession

In 1776 the remains of more than twenty stolen dead bodies were discovered in a shed in Tottenham Court Road, believed to have been left there by grave-robbers.

By 1828 grave-robbers were charging as much as 14 or even 20 guineas for a corpse. Surgeons were so concerned about rising prices that they got together and formed the Anatomy Club, to try and regulate prices and keep them down.

Some bodies were packed up and sent up to Edinburgh, where there was also a shortage of bodies for dissection. Two men called Burke and Hare had been killing people and selling their bodies to surgeons. Burke was hanged in 1832 after Hare testified against him. Hare was blinded when lime was thrown in his face (the chemical, not the citrus fruit).

The trade came to an end in 1832 – prompted by the Burke and Hare case - when a new law granted surgeons the use of the bodies of people who had died in hospital (poor people, in other words – rich people were treated at home). Unfortunately this meant that when the cholera epidemic hit London in 1832, many people refused to go to a hospital for help, in case they died and their bodies were used for dissection.

The London Connection

Even though Burke and Hare remain two of Edinburgh's most notorious criminals, it is thought that Hare, after changing his name to Mr Black, came to England and died a beggar in London.

What could people do to stop graves being robbed?

· They couldn't rely on the law – grave-robbing wasn't illegal.

· They hired private guards – but the guards could be bribed.

· They put watchers in watchtowers – but the watchers couldn't see the grave-robbers in the darkness (and they could be bribed, too).

· They hired dogs – but dogs could be beaten (or bribed with food).

· They bought heavy iron cages to be put over the grave. These were called mort-safes (mort is the French word for death) – but they cost a lot of money and you had to be rich to afford one.

· They got together and bought Parish mort-safes (also known as jankers) to be shared after funerals – but there weren't enough of them for everyone.

· Why couldn't they just cremate the bodies?

· The first crematorium wasn't built in England until 1879. (Cremation wasn't even declared legal until 1884.)

The body-snatching Borough Boys

The Borough Boys were a grave-robbing gang based in Southwark, South London, in the 1800s. They sold bodies to St Thomas's and Guy's Hospital and even sent some up to Edinburgh.

Their leader was Ben Crouch, the son of a Guy's Hospital carpenter. Before he turned to grave-robbing, he earned his living from another occupation with high risks and high rewards – he was a bare-knuckle fighter, taking part in bloody boxing matches staged in taverns for prize money.

Ben made so much money as a grave-robber that he bought a hotel in Margate and retired there. He was replaced as the leader by Patrick Murphy who, like Burke, was an Irishman. Joseph Naples, a grave-digger at St James's in Clerkenwell, was also a member of the gang.

Bishop and Williams and the Well

John Bishop was a grave-robber for twelve years, stealing and selling up to 1,000 bodies between 1799 and 1831. Late one night in November 1831, John Bishop called at King's College in the Strand with a drunk man called James May, who the night before had been seen in the Fortune of War tavern trying to wash bits of flesh off some teeth he'd taken from a corpse.

John Bishop was trying to sell a body to the recently opened King's College medical school for 12 guineas. 'Do you want anything?' he asked, as he knocked at the door. A price of 9 guineas was finally agreed, and John Bishop returned with the lifeless body of a boy of fourteen in a hamper. The boy hadn't been buried, he had a cut on his face and he had died of a blow to the back of the neck about two days before.

Anatomy instructor Richard Partridge was immediately suspicious. He pretended he needed change for a £50 note and slipped out to alert the police.

John Bishop and another grave-robber called Thomas Williams had drowned the boy, a woman and another boy in a well in John Bishop's garden in Bethnal Green. The woman, whose name was Frances Pigburn, was sold for 8 guineas to St Thomas's hospital. The other boy, who was about ten or eleven years old and whose name was Cunningham, had been sleeping under some rubbish in the pig market in Smithfield when they took him home and killed him. They sold him for 8 guineas to St Bartholomew's Hospital.

The victims were all poor, hungry and homeless, and had been taken back to John Bishops's house, fed, given rum mixed with laudanum (a form of opium) and then drowned in the well.

Bishop and Williams were hanged outside Newgate Prison in

December 1831 in front of an angry crowd of 30,000. Three people were trampled to death in the crush.

John Bishop's body was taken to King's College to be dissected, and Thomas Williams went to John Hunter's School of Anatomy in Windmill Street.

Grave-robbing was a peculiar occupation because the grave-robbers were stealing things that didn't belong to anyone, according to the law. It wasn't illegal but it disgusted people. Although it disgusted people, it provided large numbers of corpses that the surgeons needed to teach their students, many of whom went on to help sick and needy people, and to make discoveries that would advance medical science.

The strangest thing of all was that, as soon as the surgeons had enough corpses to practise on, after 1832, the grave-robbers went back to whatever job they had been doing before, or they retired on the money they had made, and the whole sorry situation ended.

CHAPTER SIX

Poisoners

'A poison in a small dose is a medicine, and a medicine in a large dose is a poison'

Alfred Swaine Taylor

Alfred Swaine Taylor should have known, he was an expert who was called to give evidence against poisoners in court during the 1800s. You probably know that medicines can harm or even kill you if you take too much of them – that's why there are child-proof caps on medicine bottles. Another person who seemed to know a lot about the subject was Dr Crippen.

Dr Crippen

Dr Crippen met a woman called Ethel when he was working as a dentist at the Yale Tooth Specialist Company in Oxford Street. Unfortunately he was still married to Cora.

Friends called in the police when Cora disappeared in February 1910 and Ethel went to a ball wearing one of Cora's brooches.

The police discovered the remains of Dr Crippen's second wife Cora in July 1910 in the cellar of their house in Holloway. Cora's head and skeleton were missing and have never been found. She had been poisoned with hyosine, which is used to treat travel sickness, and can cause hallucinations and death in large doses.

Dr Crippen fled by ship to Canada with Ethel, who had cut her hair off and was wearing boys' clothes, disguised as his son.

The disguise didn't fool anyone.

The captain of the ship telegraphed the police, who took a faster boat from Liverpool and were there to arrest Dr Crippen as he left the ship. It was the first time the newly installed ship's telegraph had been used to help the police intercept a criminal.

Dr Crippen was brought back to Britain and hanged in 1910.

Ethel later married an accountant.

Telegraph from Captain of SS *Montrose*:

Have strong suspicion that Crippen London Cellar Murderer and accomplice are amongst saloon passengers. Moustache shaved off, growing a beard. Accomplice dressed as a boy, voice, manner and build undoubtedly a girl.

Arsenic

Arsenic was a poison that was so easy to obtain and administer (it was almost tasteless) that it became known as 'inheritance powder' in the 1800s. That is, the motivations for murder were very often to kill a relation or spouse for an inheritance.

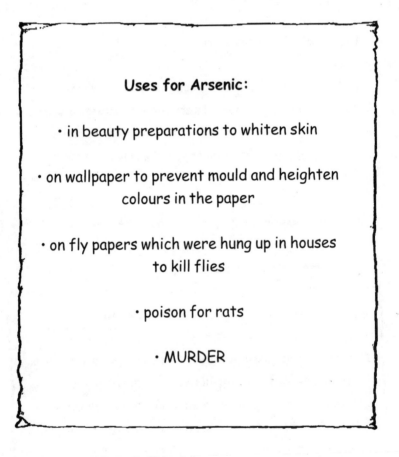

Uses for Arsenic:

• in beauty preparations to whiten skin

• on wallpaper to prevent mould and heighten colours in the paper

• on fly papers which were hung up in houses to kill flies

• poison for rats

• MURDER

An autopsy is an examination of the body of someone who has died in suspicious circumstances. To detect poison in a sample taken from the body, you have to know how chemicals will react when they are mixed with each other. The first reliable test for arsenic was developed in 1836 by chemist James Marsh, after his grandfather was poisoned with arsenic and the murderer got away with it. The test was used until the 1970s.

James Marsh's test for arsenic

Hydrochloric acid and zinc are added to the sample. The gas produced by mixing up these chemicals is put through a heated glass tube. If arsenic was present in the original sample, a brown deposit of arsenic metal will collect in the glass tube. This can be kept and shown as evidence in court.

Frederick Seddon and the fly papers

In 1910 Frederick Seddon, his wife and five children were living in a large house in London. In July they rented a room to an unmarried woman called Elizabeth Barrow, who signed over some of the things she owned to Frederick Seddon on his advice. Three months later she was dead and buried. Suspicious relatives insisted she was dug up for an autopsy, which showed she had been poisoned with arsenic. The only thing in the house that contained arsenic was a packet of fly papers, which one of the children had been sent out to buy a few weeks earlier. If Frederick Seddon had put just one fly paper in a saucepan of water and heated it up, he would have produced enough arsenic to kill a person. There was no proof that he had given Elizabeth the poison, but Frederick Seddon was the only person who profited from her death. He was found guilty of murder and hanged.

How to tell if you're being slowly poisoned by arsenic

You have white lines known as Mees lines across your fingernails, which are about 1-2mm thick

You have a peculiar bronze tint on your skin

(If your older sister has these symptoms DON'T WORRY. She's probably just wearing acrylic nails and too much blusher.)

How to tell if you've been given a large dose of arsenic

You'll have a stomach ache

Your skin will feel cold and clammy

You'll start to vomit

If you're reading this and you've got these symptoms DON'T WORRY. The other symptom I forgot to mention is:

You'll be dead within an hour ...

... and you're still here, aren't you? So that means you're OK.

George Chapman - Third Time Unlucky

You may have heard the old saying 'If at first you don't succeed, try, try and try again'. But what should you do if you succeed the first time? My advice would be – stop immediately. Especially if it's a case of murder ...

1. On Christmas Day in 1897, George Chapman's wife Mary died at the pub they ran together in East London. (OK, stop now, George. I think you got away with it. No one suspected a thing.)

2. In 1899, George married a barmaid called Bessie and they moved to a new pub, where Bessie died. (George! Stop it! Now! Stop. It. Now.)

3. George married again, and moved to yet another pub with his third wife, Maud. When Maud died in 1902, her suspicious parents paid for an autopsy which showed she had been poisoned. (Doh, too late.)

Mary and Bessie's bodies were exhumed, and tests showed that they had also been poisoned.

George Chapman (whose name, it turned out, wasn't even George Chapman, it was Severin Klosowski) was found guilty of murdering all three of his wives and hanged in 1903.

Frances Howard, Countess of Essex

Frances was married to the Earl of Essex in 1606 when she was only about thirteen years old. But Frances fell in love with Robert, Viscount Rochester, and wanted to marry him instead. After her first marriage was annulled, a man called Sir Thomas Overbury tried to put a stop to her second marriage with Robert. Frances managed to get Thomas imprisoned in the Tower of London in 1613.

She arranged for arsenic to be put in his food

... and nitric acid

... and mercury

... and spiders

In fact, for three months, she ensured that a variety of poisons were added to everything he ate. When Thomas died, the physician who visited him said that he'd died of natural causes. Frances and Robert were married about three months later. They didn't live happily ever after. In fact, they ended up hating each other.

People in the 1700s, 1800s and even the early 1900s sometimes made their own medicines at home, using ingredients they obtained from a chemist or apothecary's shop. They consulted books full of recipes for home remedies and useful information about how to treat any eventuality, like this from a book published in 1903, for people exhibiting the symptoms of rabies:

in the case of a bite from a mad animal, tie a piece of string tightly over the infected part of the body, cut out the bite, and prevent further bleeding by putting a red-hot poker in the wound. (Ow! Don't try this at home!)

There would be information on how to remove freckles, whiten the nails, cure baldness, make toothpaste, clean ostrich feathers or take care of men's hats. Inevitably, there would be an exhaustive section on poisons, their symptoms, and how to treat the unfortunate victim.

In the case of narcotic poisoning (caused by taking laudanum or deadly nightshade, for example) the advice includes making the victim sick by tickling the throat, applying smelling salts, throwing cold water in their face and, most important of all, trying to keep the patient awake by walking them up and down (as Jonathan Wild's cell-mates tried to do when he drank laudanum). Or, if possible, by applying electricity. Electricity! I wonder if anyone ever survived these cures.

The symptoms of three strong poisons:

Strychnine

Has a strong bitter taste.

Doesn't dissolve in water.

Used in rat poison.

Within twenty minutes of taking it, the muscles contract, forcing the head back and arching the spine. The muscles jump when touched, the eyes widen and stare, the pupils enlarge. Muscle spasms interfere with breathing, resulting in death from suffocation.

Belladonna ~ Deadly Nightshade

Fashionable ladies once dropped belladonna into their eyes to make the pupils larger.

It has been used to treat scarlet fever, pneumonia, nettlerash, headaches, mumps, whooping cough and typhoid, and to enlarge the pupils during eye examinations.

In September 1916 three children were taken to hospital in London suffering from belladonna poisoning, after eating the berries of the deadly nightshade plant.

Symptoms of poisoning include giddiness, confusion, excitement, enlarged pupils, difficulty in speaking or swallowing, strange or even violent behaviour, continual movement of the hands. The face is flushed and a high fever develops, followed by drowsiness, coma and eventually death.

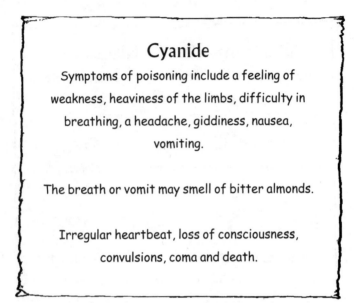

Cyanide

Symptoms of poisoning include a feeling of weakness, heaviness of the limbs, difficulty in breathing, a headache, giddiness, nausea, vomiting.

The breath or vomit may smell of bitter almonds.

Irregular heartbeat, loss of consciousness, convulsions, coma and death.

Three weird poisoning stories:

1) Georgi Markov was a Bulgarian writer who had to leave his country. He came to live in London in 1969 after criticising the Bulgarian government. As he was walking over Waterloo Bridge in September 1978, he felt a jab on his leg. A man with an umbrella apologized as he walked past. Georgi collapsed that evening and died a few days later. He'd been killed by a poison called ricin which was contained in a small pellet injected into his leg by the false tip of the umbrella. Ricin is a poison derived from castor beans, many thousands of times more toxic than cyanide. Bulgarian secret service agents were suspected of the killing, although no charges were ever brought against anyone.

2) When millionaire Whitaker Wright, one of the richest businessmen in London, was sentenced in 1903 to seven years hard labour in prison for false accounting, his reaction was to light a cigar and give away the few possessions he had with him, saying, 'I won't be needing these where I'm going.' Then he bit on a capsule of cyanide he had hidden in his mouth, killing himself before he could be taken away to prison.

3) When Edwin Bartlett died in Pimlico on New Year's Day in 1886, an autopsy showed that he had liquid chloroform in his stomach. It tastes horrible, so he wouldn't have drunk it by mistake. If he was unconscious while it was poured in his mouth, some of it would have got into his lungs but there was no trace of it there. His wife Adelaide, who was having an affair with a vicar who had bought chloroform a few days earlier, was charged with Edwin's murder but found innocent in court.

Like most people in the country, Sir James Paget - the Queen's surgeon, who was based at Bart's Hospital - followed reports of Adelaide's trial in the newspapers very closely. 'No doubt the lady was quite properly acquitted,' he said, 'but in the interests of science she should tell us how she did it.'

Poison as a weapon has always captured the public imagination because it is fairly easy to obtain, you can use it no matter how weak you are, it will kill you if even you're strong, it can be administered gradually or in one large dose, and it can be difficult to detect. Before modern forensic tests were available, there was always a chance that the murderer would get away with it! There are lots of different crime novels describing the various types of poisons available, the symptoms, and the clever detectives who catch the murderers. You've read all about the symptoms. Could you help catch a poisoner, if you ever came across one?

CHAPTER SEVEN

Bits & Pieces

Most murders are unplanned. With a dead body on their hands, people usually panic, and some of them try to get rid of the body in the hope they won't be found out. But the disposal of the body can be more messy than the murder – sometimes it's just the start of a murderer's problems!

Here are some of the ways people have tried to cover up their crimes:

Boiling

A big pot was needed for this one.

In 1879 a servant called Kate Webster threw her employer Mrs Thomas down the stairs and killed her after an argument about being sacked. Kate then cut up Mrs Thomas, boiled down the pieces, put them in a box and asked a sixteen-year-old boy to help her throw the box into the river from Richmond Bridge. She put the head in a black bag and threw it into the Thames from Hammersmith Bridge. She also offered to sell a pub landlady two jars of very rich fat, known as dripping, which comes from cooked meat and was eaten spread on bread in those days. The landlady, surprised by the size of the beast that could have produced so much fat, refused the offer. Kate Webster was arrested and sentenced to death.

Burying

Sounds simple? You'd think so ...

John Christie murdered his wife, six other women and a child, and buried them under the floorboards and in his shed in Notting Hill. His lodger, Timothy Evans, was hanged for the murder of one of the women (his own wife) and their child in 1949. But then another lodger found another body in 1953, and John Christie was eventually brought to justice and hanged.

When Henry Wainright shot his girlfriend Harriet Lane in 1874, he buried her in a warehouse in Whitechapel Road, which he used to make mats and brushes. When his business went bankrupt in 1875 and he had to leave the warehouse, Henry dug up the body, cut it up into ten pieces and wrapped it up in two parcels. He asked a man called Mr Stokes to help him load the parcels into a cab, to take him over the river to his brother's shop in Borough High Street. But Mr Stokes saw a human hand in one of the parcels and by the time Henry reached his brother's, the police were waiting for him. Henry Wainright was hanged in December that year.

Chopping

A good, sharp knife was needed, as well as some anatomical knowledge. It helped if the murderer was a butcher or a surgeon and knew where to cut the body so it would come apart easily. There is an element of chopping in most of the stories here.

Dissolving

Usually acid or lime (the chemical, not the fruit).

John Haigh was hanged in 1949 after killing nine people for their money, and dissolving their remains in baths of prussic acid. He became known as the Vampire of Kensington because he tried to avoid being hanged by pretending to be mad, even claiming he had drunk the blood of two of his victims. He went to the gallows anyway.

Dropping from an aeroplane

First you need to get yourself an aeroplane.

In 1949, Brian Hume stabbed to death a car dealer called Stanley Setty, cut off his head and legs and wrapped up what remained of him up in a parcel. Brian had learned to fly during the Second World War and was a member of a flying club. He hired a small private aeroplane and flew it over Essex Marshes, where he dropped the body. He was acquitted of the murder, although he later confessed to it, and went on to kill again.

Dumping in a left luggage office

John Robinson suffocated Minnie Bonati with a cushion in his office in May 1927, during an argument. He cut up her body, put it in a trunk and left it at Charing Cross Station's left luggage office, hoping his connection to her would never be discovered. After a few days the body started to smell and the police were called in. They traced the trunk to John Robinson via the shop he'd bought it from in Brixton. He had cleaned up all traces of her blood but he'd stopped for a cigarette when he finished. The police found a blood-stained matchstick in his waste-paper basket, and they charged him with Minnie's murder.

Dumping in the river

The body needs to be weighed down so that it won't float to the surface and be found. But the weights make it heavy to carry there in the first place, so you usually need an accomplice or an innocent helper. (See Kate Webster, who dumped her victim's body in the river after boiling it, above.)

Making pies

Sweeney Todd, the Demon Barber of Fleet Street, cut men's throats as well as their hair in his barber's shop in the late

1700s. His girlfriend, Margery Lovett, had a meat pie shop in nearby Bell Yard. Here are the gruesome details of their crimes.

Sweeney Todd, born in London in the 1740s, was abandoned by his

parents. As a boy, he was apprenticed to a barber, and later set up on his own. Like other barbers of his time, he shaved men and cut their hair with a long, sharp blade known as a cut-throat razor, as well as providing basic medical treatment, including blood-letting, which was believed to be very beneficial for health at the time.

The first time Sweeney Todd killed, he had been driven mad with jealousy. He cut the throat of a man whom he believed was in love with his girlfriend, Margery Lovett, and then he asked her to help him dispose of the evidence. They dragged the body into the basement of Margery's pie shop and emptied the victim's pockets of money and valuables. Sweeney cut up the body with one of his sharp knives, then Margery baked the pieces in a pie.

This proved to be such an economical way of obtaining ingredients, as well as providing a good source of money and trinkets from their victims' pockets, that soon they had turned their two businesses into a profitable factory. Sweeney specialized in cutting the throats of sailors and other people far away from home, whose families would never miss them. But his mistake was to bury the left-over bits and pieces of the bodies in the crypt of the nearby church. Soon there was a terrible smell in the neighbourhood, and people started to complain.

When their crime was discovered and they were arrested,

Margery smuggled poison into prison with her and took her own life. Sweeney Todd was hanged for murder.

The pie shop closed down.

Various versions of Sweeney Todd's life story have appeared in stories, films and a musical. Fortunately, he never actually existed. Or did he? There were reports of a barber near Fleet Street who cut a customer's throat from ear to ear in 1748 …

Margery Lovett's Delicious Home-made Pie Recipe for Busy Women

(Too busy to shop? Why not call your husband at work and ask him to bring the ingredients home for you?)

Ingredients:

10 kilos of meat

1 kilo of vegetables

A jar of dripping

salt & pepper

Method:

Chop up the meat and vegetables, place in a large pie dish, mix in the dripping, and add the salt and pepper. Put a layer of pastry on the top. (Why not decorate with a smiley face?) Put in the oven and bake for at least an hour. Best served warm.

If you like my pies, why not try my recipes for:

'Tasty Tatooed Crackling' & 'Toes in the Hole'

At least all those people made an effort to cover up what they had done.

Here are five people who didn't even really try:

1) Elizabeth Brownrigg, the mother of sixteen children, opened a private maternity hospital near Fleet Street in 1765. She took in orphan girls from a nearby workhouse to help her around the house and treated them with almost unimaginable cruelty. She made them sleep on bare floorboards without a cover, gave them nothing to eat but a piece of bread all day, beat them, locked them up in the coal hole, beat them some more, chained them to the door by the neck and generally made them suffer horribly until one of them, a girl called Mary Clifford, eventually died.

Neighbours and the pregnant women who were staying there were shocked at the condition of the girls, which none of the Brownrigg family had even tried to conceal, as if there was nothing unusual in having bleeding, starving, naked orphan girls around the house.

Elizabeth Brownrigg had even slashed at Mary Clifford's tongue with scissors when it emerged that she had asked a pregnant French woman to help her. Elizabeth Brownrigg was hanged in 1767 and then taken away for dissection.

2) George Smith, known as the Brides in the Bath murderer, bought a bath in 1912, drowned his first wife, Bessie, in it and then took it back to the shop the next day saying he didn't need it.

He drowned his second wife, Alice, in Blackpool in 1913, only four weeks after he married her. He drowned his third wife, Margaret, in London in 1914, the day after he married her.

He was eventually tracked down and sentenced to death.

3) Sarah Malcolm was twenty-two years old in 1732 when she strangled her eighty-year-old employer, Mrs Duncombe, and killed two of Mrs Duncombe's servants – Elizabeth Harrison and Alice Price, who was seventeen years old. Sarah had cut Alice's throat but she continued to deny that she was guilty, even though she had blood on her clothes, and a tankard with blood on its handle was found in her room.

Sarah attracted a great deal of interest because she denied her crimes. She was painted by a famous painter called William Hogarth when she was in prison waiting to be executed. When she was hanged near the scene of her crimes in Fetter Lane in 1733, there were so many people crowded together to watch her die that it was possible to use people's shoulders as stepping stones – one woman who tried it successfully got all the way across the street.

4) In 1865 Thomas Briggs became the first person to be murdered on a train, although he didn't know that when he boarded at Fenchurch Street Station, on his way to Hackney. Passengers getting into an empty carriage, when the train arrived at Hackney station, discovered traces of blood and a hat with an unusual flattened shape.

In those days, gentlemen always wore hats when they went out. Thomas Briggs was found dying on the tracks, unable to tell the police what had happened. The hat was the only clue to the murderer but it was a pretty good one.

It was soon traced to a German, Franz Muller. He fled to America on a sailing ship with Thomas Briggs's hat, which he'd picked up from the railway carriage by mistake, and which he'd tried to flatten, to get it into the shape he liked wearing. The police raced to America on a steam ship – which was faster than the sailing ship – and were at the docks in New York to meet Franz Muller and arrest him.

5) Jack the Ripper killed six or eight women in Whitechapel in the East End of London in the summer of 1898 (experts can't agree how many of them there were). The murderer didn't try to hide the bodies and he was never caught, although someone calling himself 'Jack the Ripper' wrote to the police several times, claiming responsibility.

The crimes remain unsolved to this day and Scotland Yard didn't close the files on the murders until nearly a hundred years later, in 1992.

There are people who have killed more than once, but they're unusual. Some of them have even got away with it ... for a while. Most of us will never commit murder, never steal, never break the law on purpose, and never lie unless it is to make another person feel better. (Even then, I don't recommend it. You tend to get caught out and everyone ends up feeling bad.) The few people in London each year who murder someone usually do it only once, and they turn out not to be very good at it. It's just as well, really, isn't it?

Why not read one (or all) of the following books?

Smith by Leon Garfield. A twelve-year-old pickpocket in London in the 1700s gets drawn into a mystery when he sees a man being killed. I loved this story when I first read it years ago and I would highly recommend it.

The Potato Factory by Bryce Courtenay. What happened to Ikey Solomon after he was arrested and transported to Australia? Bryce Courtenay is a very popular Australian writer who has mixed fact and fiction in this book.

Oliver Twist by Charles Dickens. A young orphan called Oliver joins a gang of pickpockets run by a man called Fagin. This is a funny, thrilling adventure story but it takes a while to get used to the language.

Dr Jekyll & Mr Hyde by Robert Louis Stevenson. Written in 1881, it is based on the stories of Burke & Hare, the two grave-robbers in Edinburgh who murdered people and sold their bodies.

Charles Dickens's *Tale of Two Cities*, set in 1775, included a character called Jerry Cruncher who was a grave-robber.

Why not pick up one of Agatha Christie's books and read one for yourself? They're easy to read and great fun – much better than the TV programmes based on them.

Dorothy L Sayers's Lord Peter Wimsey novel, *Strong Poison*, is a very entertaining read, and includes a description of the Marsh test for arsenic.

Here are some criminal places to visit

The Dickens House Museum, 48 Doughty Street, London WC1.
See where the great writer lived. www.dickensmuseum.com

The Museum of London, 150 London Wall, London EC2. See how
London would have looked in Jonathan Wild, Jenny Diver and
Moll Cutpurses's lifeimes. There's lots of information about
women, men and children throughout London's history.
www.museum-london.org.uk

Visit the **Royal College of Surgeons**, 35–43 Lincoln's Inn Fields,
London WC2, to see Jonathan Wild's skeleton. www.rcseng.ac.uk

The Clerkenwell House of Detention Museum, Clerkenwell
Close, London EC1. See where Jack Sheppard escaped from with
Bess Edgworth.

A visit to the **Clink Prison Museum** at Clink Street, SE1, will give
you a good idea of the conditions of the prisons that Jack
stayed in – and escaped from. www.clink.co.uk

The Victoria and Albert Museum, Cromwell Road, South
Kensington, London SW7. You'll see the kind of dresses Jenny
Diver would have worn, and try to picture how she would have
looked in her pregnancy kit with the false arms. www.vam.ac.uk

The Old Operating Theatre, Museum & Herb Garret, 9a St
Thomas Street, London SE1. This is a very interesting little
museum that is reached by walking up a spiral wooden staircase.
You'll learn how operations were performed in the 1800s, about

herbs used in medicines and a little bit about the grave-robbers who supplied the hospital's surgeons with dead bodies. www.thegarret.co.uk

The Hunterian Museum at The Royal College of Surgeons (see above). A lot of the exhibits were destroyed by bombing during the Second World War, so you won't see the skeletons of the giraffes or elephants. But there are things like pickled hands and monkey paws in jars, the pickled brain of Charles Babbage (who invented computers) and the skeletons of Jonathan Wild and the Irish Giant, Charles Byrne. Some of the things are quite gruesome and it's not the sort of museum you can run around in and press buttons or levers, like the Science Museum. It's fascinating, though. Go and visit if you can. www.rcseng.ac.uk

Madame Tussaud's Waxworks, Marylebone Road, London NW1. This famous attraction often has long queues but if you decide to visit, have a look in the Chamber of Horrors for some of the people I've mentioned. www.madame-tussauds.com

The London Dungeon, 28-34 Tooley Street, SE1. At this popular museum near London Bridge you can experience the gruesome Jack the Ripper tour, as well as many other crimes and punishments served up in this book. www.thedungeons.com

If you enjoyed this book, why not try others in the series:

CRYPTS, CAVES AND TUNNELS OF LONDON
by Ian Marchant
Peel away the layers under your feet and discover
the unseen treasures of London beneath the streets.
ISBN 1-904153-04-6

RATS, BATS, FROGS AND BOGS OF LONDON
by Chris McLaren
Find out where you can find some of the amazing species
London has to offer the budding naturalist.
ISBN 1-904153-05-4

DUNGEONS, GALLOWS AND SEVERED HEADS OF LONDON
by Travis Elborough
For spine-chilling tortures and blood-curdling punishments,
not to mention the most revolting dungeons and prisons you
can imagine.
ISBN 1-904153-03-8

THE BLACK DEATH AND OTHER PLAGUES OF LONDON
by Natasha Narayan
Read about some of the most vile and rampant diseases ever
known and how Londoners overcame them – or not!
ISBN 1-904153-01-1

GHOSTS, GHOULS AND PHANTOMS OF LONDON
by Travis Elborough
Meet some of the victims of London's bloodthirsty monarchs,
murderers, plagues, fires and famines - who've chosen to stick
around!
ISBN 1-904153-02-X

In case you have difficulty finding any Watling St books in your local bookshop, you can place orders directly through

BOOKPOST
Freepost
PO Box 29
Douglas
Isle of Man
IM99 1BQ

Telephone: 01624 836000
e-mail: bookshop@enterprise.net